DATE DUE

JUL 19 2000			
			Printed in USA

HIGHSMITH #45230

With an Aborigine at Melville Island. The man is in a ceremonial period when he can not touch food so must be fed by another.

←

Harney with Dr. Frank Setzler of the Smithsonian Institute at Yirrkala. (1948 Smithsonian-National Geographic Expedition)

↓

Harney interrogating an old native near a Leichardt memorial on the Roper River.

↑

A member of the Waradgery Tribe finds a succulent witchetty grub in a eucalyptus tree

←

WILLIAM E. HARNEY

Bill and anthill. ↑

In a cave at Oenpelli, West
↓ Arnhem Land, eating flying
fox with Aboriginals.

With the National Geographic
Expedition to Melville Is. 1954 ↑

Front: Dr. Jane C. Goodale and
C.P. Mountford

Back: George Joy, Brian Daly,
and Bill Harney

YARNS FROM AN AUSSIE BUSHCOOK

BiLL HARNEY'S COOK BOOK

YARNS from an AUSSIE BUSHCOOK

Bill Harney

in collaboration with
Patricia Thompson

COBBERS BOOKS

a division of
Martensen Company Inc.
Farmington, Michigan

YARNS FROM AN AUSSIE BUSHCOOK, Copyright © 1979 by

The Martensen Company Inc. All rights reserved. No part of
this book may be used or reproduced in any manner whatsoever
without the written permission of the Martensen Company Inc.
For information address COBBERS Books, The Martensen
Company Inc., 22725 Orchard Lake Road, Farmington, Michigan 48024

First edition. Printed in Michigan, U.S.A.

Library of Congress Card No. 79-55363
ISBN #0-934680-00-0

Photographs courtesy of Mr. Douglas Lockwood, Bendigo, Victoria, Australia. Front cover coordinated by Jan Denny.

1st published as "Bill Harney's Cookbook" in Australia, 1960.

For all of Bilarney's cobbers
past, present, and future

CONTENTS

ABOUT THIS BOOK

and the bushman called Bilarney

Australia was my home for nearly twelve years, and I am the richer for it. That compelling giant land has produced independent folk who live life with dignity and good cheer. They reconciled a harsh lonely bushland with a highly civilized heritage and built some of the world's most beautiful cities. Along the way, they created a cosmopolitan culture yielding great artists and musicians, sportsmen and chefs.

Yet today, the outback remains almost unchanged from the vast remote arid country that was there when the first European settlers arrived. Studied by scientists, rich in mineral resources, it endures as the legendary land of the Back of Beyond. The Bush.

I first saw this little book in Adelaide, South Australia. A tall stack of them was being autographed by a man obviously well-known. He was stocky, white-haired with vivid blue eyes, surrounded by smiling people, talking non-stop. Curious, I picked up "Bill Harney's Cookbook" and was captivated. How unique as a gift for the folks back home! I mentioned my find to journalist neighbors and was invited promptly to their home to meet none other than—Bill Harney.

It was one of the most memorable evenings of my life. Bill had a bewitching enthusiasm for life and profound knowledge about people in the bush country. Best of all, he loved to talk...and to listen. He was curious about American Indian cooking and about clambakes, all so similar to methods used by some Australian Aborigines and Polynesian islanders.

We were spellbound with stories of the native foods that he had learned to cook and to eat. "Why not witchetty grubs? The French eat snails, a very like taste. I hear that the Arabs eat toasted locusts. And the colonists over in New Caledonia think flying fox are bonza (great) cooked in red wine." Facts were laced with adventures and always his stories pointed to a humor in man groping to adjust to his environment.

Born the son of a roaming Queensland miner, young Bill had a few short years of formal education before 'going bush'. Variously, he was a drover, camp cook, trader in trepang and pearlshell. He went to Europe with the AEF, returned to the Northern Territory bushland and became a cattleman, always reading, reading, where-ever there were books, storing quotes and information. He roamed again as a native affairs patrol officer, a government advisor on aborigine affairs—and a writer and storyteller. As his fame spread, and his love of talking became known, he was asked to make broadcasts for the ABC and for the BBC in London. It was in London that he purchased his first suit: he was 60 years old.

In 1948, Bill's services were sought as guide and advisor for the joint National Geographic Society—Smithsonian Institute—Commonwealth of Australia expedition study-ing stone-age Arnhem Land in Northeast Australia. As chronicled in the December 1949 issue of National Geo-graphic: "His (Harney's) knowledge of Arnhem Land, especially the coast of the Gulf of Carpenteria, is phenomenal; of the aborigine people, deep understanding; of the fauna and flora, remarkable. As storyteller, poet, and singer, Bill amused everyone with his tales of the country, of drovers and cattle thieves, of journeys among black fellows, and he sang rollicking songs of stockmen..."

Another member of that expedition was Dr. Robert R. Miller, ichthyologist, now Curator of Fishes for the Museum of Zoology and Professor of Biological Sciences at the University of Michigan. When contacted recently, his first response was "That wonderful man! No one who meets him forgets Bill Harney." Dr. Miller has a special photo of Bill. The expedition leader had wanted to document photographically a sequence of Aborigines constructing a dug-out canoe; the particular tribe then being studied had forgotten the skills...so, Bilarney re-taught those stone-age Aborigines. Suitably photographed, of course.

In 1954, there was another expedition, this one to Melville Island in the Northern Territory. Bilarney was again guide and mentor, as reported in the March 1956 article in the National Geographic magazine. Accompanying that expedition was Dr. Jane C. Goodale, now Professor of Anthropology at Bryn Mawr College, who writes, "Bill was perhaps the most remarkable of persons to have influenced my life. Without his friendship and insights into the Aboriginal world, my first professional field trip...could have been in no way as personally satisfying as it was. Bill had the ability to transmit friendship and respect to all mankind, for he was at once interested and curious about everything and everyone. A brilliant story teller, he was a superb listener as well; kind and generous of his time and knowledge. By example, he taught me that anthropology is first a humanistic discipline and then a social science, and that respect and friendship are the two most important tools of the field worker in anthropology...I wish that more of his works were available here."

(Pub. Note: As soon as possible. He wrote 12 books.)

Another American friend, Carleton S. Coon, anthropologist, former professor at Harvard and the University of Pennsylvania, author of THE ORIGIN OF RACES, writes, "Bill was the anthropologists' anthropologist who had been out with almost everyone who was studying the Aborigines, because he was the number one authority without a rival. He could speak I have no idea how many native languages but could talk to all of them in pidgin. He knew exactly how to handle them. Once when two men came to him to settle a quarrel, he said 'Him blackfella business, him no whitefella business,' and sent them away...He was exceedingly sensitive to every nuance of speech or behavior, but outwardly bland..."

It was during that Melville Island expedition that a revered American arrived in Australia. The story is related beautifully by Douglas Lockwood in his book CROCODILES AND OTHER PEOPLE. Lockwood at that time was the National Territory correspondent for the prestigious Melbourne HERALD: "In the 1950's a distinguished American jurist and inveterate traveller, Justice William O. Douglas of the U.S. Supreme Court, visited Darwin. I was at the aerodrome when he landed...and (I) wanted to know why a man whose name had been mentioned as a possible contender for the Presidency would want to waste time in a frontier town like Darwin.

"I've heard of a man named William E. Harney," the Judge said. "Some of my friends at the Smithsonian told me if I was going around the world I should make Harney one of my stopping places."

I told the Judge that Bill was camped by Snake Bay, about 100 miles away on the northern tip of Melville. "Is there an aerodrome?" he asked. There was. "Perhaps they've got a charter plane here?" They had. And Justice Douglas chartered it and flew off to Snake Bay. I told him that Bill was a close family friend. He promised to see me on his return.

When the plane came back three days later it had not one passenger but two. William O. Douglas and William E. Harney.

I knew that Bill was under contract as an advisor on aboriginal affairs to an Australian ethnologist, Charles P. Mountford, who was studying the Tiwi tribesmen. "What are you doing here?" I asked.

'I'm with the Judge."
"What about Mountford?"
"He's given me leave for a fortnight...The Judge wants me to go down the track to Alice Springs with him. (1000 miles.)
"Why?"
"Just to talk to him."

I've seldom seen such an eminent man so completely captivated as the Judge. Bill turned to him and said, "What did we have for breakfast this morning?" "Turtle egg omelette," Douglas said. "Correct. And for dinner last night?" "Fried flying fox," the Judge said, delighted.

A few hours later, in equally high spirits, they began a road trip to Alice Springs. When Bill returned he was full of the Judge's wonderful yarns, but he must have told a few himself. He opened his spectacles case, which many bushmen use as a wallet, and showed me a cheque signed William O. Douglas. Four hundred dollars. Payee: William E. Harney. I was envious. . .(that) was then a lot of money in Northern Australia. . ."What for?" "Just for talking," Bill said. "Plenty more where that came from, he reckons, if only I'd go on a lecture tour of the United States."

Bill never made a lecture tour of the States. He travelled to London and made a history of sorts in his talks for the BBC, then became busy tending Ayers Rock, the great monolith of sandstone in Central Australia, as Curator and resident bush personality. Until, one summer's day, his great heart wore out. His wife, daughter and son had predeceased him. . .but Bill's extensive knowledge of his country and its people with the warmth of his humor is recorded in his books.

Here, then, are some of Bilarney's bush recipes and bush stories. Enjoy the flavor of each.

Jean Martensen
Publisher and Editor
COBBERS Books

I

Cooks, Cuckoos and Wilful Murderers

The babbling brook*
The shovel took
The damper to unfold.
"Another sod?
So help me God
That beats the flaming world!"

—Old Bush Ballad.

THERE IS AN old joke in the outback that a man is not considered a good bush cook unless he can make tasty soup out of a pair of old socks. It is indeed marvellous what an experienced man can turn into good tucker, and such a man gets a great reputation. There was a cook known far and wide along the Georgina as The Old Tropical Frog, who was famous for his skill in turning scanty and unpromising ingredients into tasty meals.

Cooking in the bush is, in its own way, a real art. The good cook studies the wind, when it blows and from what direction, so that he knows the best times in which to get his work done. If he finds that a strong wind usually comes up at ten o'clock in the morning, he knows he has to get his bread cooked as early as possible. He knows how to make

* Bush term for cook.

a wind-break to protect his fire; he has to know all about the various woods, their heat content and whether they are suitable to use on his fire, for good wood is essential to proper bush cookery.

Bush cooks argue a great deal about the sort of wood one should use. There was one man travelling with the drovers who would stay and cook for them as long as they were among the gidgee wood. As soon as the gidgee cut out, away he would go: He refused to cook a damper on any other sort of wood. Other cooks will only make damper when they are able to get quinine bush for their fires.

As the cook is continually travelling with the drovers and cattlemen, the kind of water he will find at each camp is vitally important to him. Sometimes the waterholes are muddy; he has to know how to get the water clear. If he is in a hurry, he will mix a couple of spoonfuls of flour into a kerosene tin full of water. The flour settles the mud at the bottom of the tin. Sometimes he uses the native method of throwing ashes into the tin, as wood ash will also carry the sediment to the bottom.

At Newcastle Waters, in the Northern Territory, the water from the big Malindji waterhole was murky. The native women used to bring it up to the station and pour it into 40-gallon drums. Into each drum they put some Epsom salts, which purified two-thirds of the water, leaving behind a one-third sediment of mud.

The bush cook also has to know how to cope with flies. He cannot make stews in the fly time because it will give the men "Barcoo." And if he wants to make a mince, he has to grind his meat at night and put it into the camp oven before the flies get busy next day.

There is a proper way of carrying suet in the bush; you put it into the flour sack, so that it won't go sour. Similarly, if you are carrying tins of butter, you have to put the tins in with the corned beef, because in that way it will keep cool.

The placing of cooking pots alongside the fire is very important. Which side of the fire is hottest? Where will the billy boil most quickly? Some cooks are for the windward side, some for the lee side. In the bush it is not unusual for bets to be laid on which billy will boil the fastest, and much money is won and lost.

Certain men are supposed to have champion billy cans and cooking pots, and one man I knew won the Quart-Pot Boiling Championship for three years running. The contestants would stand ready with their cooking pots, and at a given signal they would start their fires, put their pots to boil, and throw in the tea when the water reached boiling point. Contests like this were widely held in Camooweal and other bush towns.

There is an old saying in the bush that when you have a good cook, your battle is already won. The bush cook can be a very valuable man indeed. Not only does he provide good tucker, he has to be a good storyteller who is able to keep the men happy by telling them yarns. Everything goes merrily in the camp that has a good cook. Such a man has usually been a stockman and cattleman in his youth, and has taken to the cooking because he is getting old. He becomes something of a wise man, or glee man.

Woe betide the camp where the cook is a nark! By the very nature of his calling, the cook is brought constantly into touch with a number of people with very different temperaments, and a man of touchy temper sometimes becomes very temperamental as a result. Bad-tempered cooks are known as "adders."

The men sometimes divide them into three classes — cooks, cuckoos and wilful murderers. For a joke, they will refer to their cook as "the bait-layer." Personal nicknames are legion, and have become part of the history of the outback.

I well remember The Wooden Owl, so-called because he got on with his cooking and said not a word to anybody. However, he was a great curry man, and his services were much in demand. Then there was old Short Stop who, of course, did not stop long in any one place. He would turn out grand food for a while and then disappear over-night, leaving a note to tell the boss where to send his cheque. Another got the name of Sitting Shot. One night he had a row with a drover, who sacked him while he was lying in his swag. He complained that the drover was no sport, to take a sitting shot at an old bird in the nest: And the nickname stuck. Sitting Shot's great speciality was the making of particularly delicious rock cakes.

One of the great bread cooks of the country was called The Speckled Hen, on account of his freckles.

Sometimes the cooks were famous for their failures. There was one who became known far and wide as Mud Spring. I must explain that, in the back country, the mantle of rock that covers the artesian waters sometimes faults, and the water seeps upwards to form springs on the surface of the ground.

These springs form thick patches of mud in the black soil, surrounded by bulrushes. The pressure of water beneath causes the mud springs to rise into mounds, perhaps 15ft. or 20ft. across and 4ft. high. Now this cook used to have a lot of failures at yeast bread, and he was wont to bury his failures in the ground. Naturally, the yeast went on working, and the bread dough kept on rising, and his burial grounds were real traps of festering moist dough. One day the boss, walking around the camp, sank up to his knees in a rotting mess of yeast, just as the unwary might sink into the slushy mess of a mud spring. The boss flew into a rage and sacked the cook on the spot—and that's how he got his nickname, Mud Spring.

Long wire hooks, used for lifting the lids off camp ovens and billy cans, are the bush cook's badge of office. He is never seen without them. He ties them carefully together at one end, or fixes pieces of calico on each one, so that he will not lose them. A good cook never loses his hooks, but if he has a row with the boss, he gives notice like this: "Well, if that's how you feel about it, here's me hooks. I'm headin'."

Several bushmen have come down in history as great damper makers. In the 'twenties, Micky Coleman was considered to be one of the best damper cooks of the Georgina. We all wanted to know what his secret was. Some reckoned it was just the touch he had with the dough, others claimed that he put a little sugar in it. We eventually learned his secret. He made his dough very soft, then greased his camp oven and let the dough stand in it for about 15 minutes so that the rising would work. When the dough began to rise, Micky would put the oven gently on the coals and cover the lid with hot ashes. In the result, he produced a damper with the consistency of yeast bread or light sponge cake — it was wonderful!

All the fine points of making good damper, what rising to use, what wood is best, what temperature the fire should reach, and so on — these are quite as serious and important to the bush cook as discussions on fine sauces are to city chefs.

Naturally there is an aristocracy among bush cooks. The drovers' cook is not in the same line of country as the head cook at the station who is often something of a chef. He, they say, cooks for Government House — meaning the station owner and his family.

Some of the men who go out cooking for the drovers and the musterers get a longing for a bit of town life. Such a one was old Blue Bob of Borroloola. He'd complain that "his skin was crackin' for want of a drink," and his main joy when he finally did get to town was to run up and down the street snorting like a horse and calling on the police to "yard" him!

Cooking bread and damper

2

Bread, Damper and Other Recipes

Though torn is my tent and my bed is a sack,
I pity that cove with a swag on his back,
From rush to new rush away scampers he,
While I'm here snugly taking my damper and tea.
                                        —V. S. Raphael.

ONCE, DAMPERS WERE simply made in the ashes. The cook would make a big fire, and when only white-hot ashes were left, the damper was cooked by scraping aside the hot coals with a long stick and carefully laying the dough in the heart of the fire, making sure first that the dough was not more than 2in. thick. (Keeping it thin facilitated quick and good baking.) Then the coals and ashes already scraped aside were heaped over the dough, and the lot was made airtight to prevent burning. When the damper was cooked, the ashes had to be scraped and brushed off.

Nowadays, dampers are made in camp ovens. These used to be three-legged pots made of cast iron, but they have been largely supplanted by Bedourie ovens, which were first made in West Queensland. Bedourie ovens are made of steel, so that you could put a Bedourie on a packhorse and, if the horse bucked and threw its pack, the steel oven would not break as the old brittle cast-iron pots did.

They have always argued in the outback about the best sort of rising to use in dampers. In Borroloola and other outback towns, the cream of tartar was sometimes left out of the cargo or loading from the teams or ships. At once the controversy would start afresh: How best to make dampers? (Strictly speaking, I suppose, one should limit the term "damper" to the plain flour and water mixture. When rising was added, it was known as "light bread." But these days, rising is universally added, though the old bushies always claim that light bread never sticks to their ribs the way the good old heavy damper did.)

It's a bit of an art to make the bread rise without cream of tartar and baking soda. Some used to say that if you used pot liquor (water in which corned beef had been cooked) with a little of the fat left floating in it, kneaded the dough up very quickly and threw it on the coals, the damper would rise slightly. Others claimed that soda alone would make it rise a bit, and someone discovered that a bit of vinegar in the water, with soda, was quite effective. But no one seemed to fancy the brownish colour which the vinegar lent to the bread!

I remember when Cliff Lynott, storekeeper at Borroloola, made his great discovery. He found that Eno's Fruit Salts made a damper rise beautifully. He was so pleased that he sent a testimonial to Eno's factory in England, telling them that their Salts were in great demand in the Australian outback for breadmaking. He was amazed when he never got a reply!

In places where there might not be deliveries of food stores for three or four months, people had to learn to rely on the bush to keep alive. As supplies of flour ran low, station hands and bushmen fell back on native food. They learned — especially in the Borroloola district — how to grind up the nuts of the cycad palm for flour.

The natives have always used these nuts, which are about 1in. in diameter. When cracked open they have a nice fresh kernel. (The natives sliced these kernels with the sharp edge of a kangaroo's bladebone.) The sliced nuts were dried in the sun for two days and then stored in big bags. When they were wanted, the natives soaked the nuts in water to wash out the poisonous acid, and then ground them between two big flat stones. The flour thus obtained can be used for making dampers.

The natives call the nuts of the cycad palm Munja or Nargueamma, and they like to make big cakes of the flour, at least 3in. thick.

The bushies didn't like the way the natives treated the Munja. Being soaked in cold water, the nuts fermented and gave off a fearful smell. Leichhardt the explorer complained that Munja bread smelt like very old German cheese.

However, the nuts obviously had food value, and flour was desperately short, and someone found out that if the kernels were obtained from the natives before soaking, the odour was not nearly so bad. The white men simply soaked the nuts in two lots of boiling water, and the poison (a milky substance) ran out. They then used half wheat flour and half palm flour. As wheat flour ran lower still, they increased the proportion of palm flour. Finally, they had to use palm flour alone.

Oddly enough, the worse the native bread smells, the better it tastes, like some old cheeses. Leichhardt was quite right in his comparison.

I often make damper when I am away in the bush. Before describing some variations, here is a good reliable basic recipe.

DAMPER. Take 3lb. of flour and chuck it into a dish, put a bit of salt to it and some rising, in the proportion of 2 cream of tartar to 1 bicarbonate of soda. For a 3lb. damper, use 1oz. of cream of tartar to ½oz. of soda. Pour some water into the dish and mix it well into a light dough.

Now sprinkle a little flour over the bottom of the camp oven to prevent the damper sticking, put in the dough, and put the lid on top. To cook, you must have ready a shallow hole in the ground, into which hot ashes are placed with a shovel*. Put the camp oven over the hot ashes, then cover it completely with more hot ashes. It must be completely covered, otherwise it will burn. After about half an hour, lift the lid with a pair of wire hooks, scrape off the ashes, and tap the camp oven with a stick. If it gives off a hollow sound, the damper is cooked.

If you wish to keep the damper for some time, and the weather is dry, rub it with a little fat from corned beef. This will keep it soft.

JOHNNY CAKES. These are simply small dampers, made about as big as the palm of your hand, and patted very thin. The mixture is the same as above, of course. Spread the fire well out and put the Johnny Cakes on top of the hot coals. After about two minutes, turn them over. They swell up nicely.

* A shovel is an absolute necessity for a bush cook.

When cooked, they should be tossed on to some leaves. They should be eaten straight away; don't cut them, break them with the fingers as you would break open a freshly-made scone. To keep them fresh, put them into a tin before they are really cold. If allowed to dry out, they become as hard as bricks.

Bushmen make Johnny Cakes if they are in a hurry, or too hungry to wait for a proper Damper. For the same reason, they will sometimes make Dumplings, or Sinkers.

SINKERS. Using the same basic dough as above, make it into rounds about the size of a tennis ball. Put them into the boiling stewpot, or into boiling water with a bit of fat on top of it which helps to seal the dough. Boil for 15 minutes. Sinkers are usually served hot with golden syrup.

BUSH PLUM PUDDING. To 3lb. of flour add a little salt, cream of tartar (1oz.) and baking soda (½oz.). Shred into it 4oz. of suet, and add ½lb. of sugar, some grated or cut-up lemon peel, currants and raisins to taste. Make into a wet mixture with burnt-sugar water (made by burning sugar in a pan until almost black and then dissolving it in water). Put the mixture into a greased cloth and tie the top with string. Put into a tin of boiling water and boil for four hours. When it is cooked, take it out, pour cold water over the cloth, untie the string and roll the pudding out on to a dish, when it is ready to serve.

A SAUCE can be made with milk, cornflour (or ordinary flour), a pinch of salt and a little sugar. If you have no milk, add golden syrup to the water and thicken with cornflour as above.

BROWNIE (BUSH PLUM CAKE). To 2lb. of flour, to which rising has been added, put two or three good spoonfuls of fat, which should be rubbed thoroughly into the flour. Add sugar to taste, and plenty of currants and raisins. Add sufficient water to make a nice soft dough. Grease the inside of the camp oven thoroughly, scrape in the dough and cook like a Damper (see above). It is possible to cook Brownies on the coals, but unlike Dampers they must be wrapped up in several thicknesses of paper, otherwise the fat will cause the mixture to run.

If bush cooks are a bit mean with the fruit in Plum Puddings or Brownies, the drovers tell them not to stand 100 yards off to throw in the fruit.

A plain Damper mixture is sometimes broken into small pieces and fried in fat; the resulting scones are called Puftaloons.

Here is a dish known as Fat Cattle Drovers' Plum Pudding, or, more picturesquely, as SPOTTED SLUT. Cook a sufficient quantity of rice, and when it is ready, throw in a couple of hand-fuls of raisins and sufficient sugar to sweeten it. Continue cooking until the rice is dry.

The following is an outback version of beef with dumplings, with an odd name:

BUSH SEA PIE. Cut up beef and onions, and anything else you may have in camp which will make the stew tasty. Add salt and pepper, and boil it in the camp oven until the beef is tender. Have ready some Damper mixture rolled out to a thickness of about ½in. Put this over the stew about 15 minutes before serving. (Bush cooks slip in the Damper when they hear the men riding back through the bush.)

When the meat supply runs out, bushmen find rice and onion stew tasty. I've also had this dish on sailing boats and, for that matter, all along the coast. You simply boil up the rice, add plenty of onions and a spoonful of fat, and salt and pepper to taste. It goes down very well when you're hungry.

BUSH MEAT PUDDING. (For 3 people). Cut up 1½lb. of chuck steak very small; take 3 carrots, 2 potatoes and 2 onions, wash, peel and cut them up. (Use other vegetables or flavourings as desired.) Add the vegetables to the meat, pepper and salt to taste, and mix well. Now take a pint measure of flour and 2 teaspoons of baking powder or its equivalent in cream of tartar and bicarbonate of soda.* Mix up all the ingredients just like a pudding, add a little water, and when it is the same consistency as a plum pudding, tie it up and boil it for 3 or 4 hours.

Another method is to make a dough (using the Damper mixture, of course), but adding some salt and a little fat. Roll out the dough and spread the meat and vegetables over it. Roll up again like a jam roll and tie it up in a piece of greased calico. Sew up the ends, and boil as above.

Bush Meat Pudding or Roll is very good served with an Onion Sauce.

BUSH RISSOLES. Cooked corned beef is finely shredded and mixed with pepper, and finely chopped onions, flour, soda and cream of tartar. The batter is dropped by spoonfuls into hot fat, and fried until golden brown.

DRY CURRY made with cooked meat. Put a little butter or fat into a frying pan, and in this brown

* Owing to the humidity in the bush, baking powder sometimes becomes spoilt. To test it, put a spoonful in cold water. If it fizzes, it is good. Otherwise it might as well be thrown away.

some sliced onions. Add curry powder to suit the taste. Into this mixture put cubes of meat. Mix and heat well. Then add a little flour, and when it has browned, add some lemon juice and a little water. Stir and serve. (If fresh meat is used, it should be cut very small and cooked with the onions before the curry powder is added.)

RICE FOR CURRY. Take five parts of rice and wash thoroughly in two waters, or until the rice flour has gone. Now add a little salt and dry the rice in a saucepan with the lid on, over the fire. Add eight parts of boiling water to the heated rice, and boil until dry on surface (about 8 minutes), then continue to cook slowly until the rice is perfectly dry.

BURDEKIN DUCKS (or Kimberley Oysters). Use either cold or corned beef. First cut the meat into slices, then make a batter of flour, baking powder, milk or water, and finely chopped onions. Beat the batter well, dip each slice into it and fry in hot fat until the fritters are golden brown.

BUSHMAN'S STEW (or Drover's Stew). For six people, take 3lb. of cold corned beef and cut it into pieces, setting the fat aside. Add cut up potatoes and pumpkin, or other vegetables. Cover with water, bring to the boil and simmer until the vegetables are cooked. Let it cool a little, then thicken it with 3 spoonfuls of flour (and a spoonful of curry, perhaps) well mixed with cold water. Cover, and let it simmer slowly at the side of the fire for a few minutes. The drovers used to find this stew far tastier than one made with fresh meat.

BUSH POTATO PIE. Mince cold roast or corned beef, add some chopped onions and a little bacon, a dab of butter, salt and pepper, and put into the camp oven. Add some water and spread over it mashed potato. Bake until the potato covering is brown (about 1 hour). Serve with tomato sauce.

BUSH ROLY-POLY. Make a dough of 2 cups of flour, cream of tartar and soda 2 to 1 (or baking powder), some shredded suet, sugar and salt. Roll the dough to a thickness of a third of an inch. Spread with jam or golden syrup which has been well mixed with breadcrumbs, roll up carefully and place it in a piece of greased calico. Tie the ends and sew along the edge of the calico. Put into boiling water and boil for 3 hours.

Note: If you have no suet, ordinary beef dripping can be used, but the pudding must not be overcooked, as it will go soggy — which it will not do if made with suet.

Never use flint

3

Birds, Beef and Bandicoots

So stir the Wallaby Stew,
  Make soup with the Kangaroo tail,
I tell you things is pretty tough,
  Since Dad got put in jail

—Old Bush Ballad.

NATURALLY, IN THE bush a lot of the meat is cooked in the same way as in the cities. The camp oven is used like an ordinary oven, and the meat is stewed or roasted, grilled or fried, as desired.

But where there are no camp ovens, or the camp oven is too small for the quantity of meat to be cooked, we revert to the ground oven of the Aborigines.

A ground oven is made in the following manner: According to the size of the piece of beef, a hole is scooped out of the ground. For a piece weighing about 10lb., a hole about 4in. deep, 12in. wide and 18in. long is needed, scooped out into the shape of a shallow dish. In this shallow hole, a wood fire is lighted. It is important that the right kind of wood is used. Quinine wood and gidgees burn nicely, and will not give off a bad flavour; paper barks are excellent and so is the wood of the red river gum. On the other hand, dogwood, macrocarpa and leopard woods give the meat a very unpleasant taste.

The wood, then, is placed in the hole and lighted, and a number of stones are put into the fire to heat up. Here again it is necessary to be careful. Never use flint, which cracks and explodes. Granite stones are very good. Failing stones, use broken-up ant-bed, suitably cleaned of course.

With this type of cooking, it is always advisable to have the skin still on the meat. It helps to keep the flavour and juices of the meat intact.

The fire has burned down, the stones are red-hot, and now it is time to begin your cooking. Branches of grevillea (the bottle brush) or red river gum have been picked ready, and soaked in water. Over the red-hot stones place these wet branches, and as they steam, put the beef on them, skin or selvedge side down. Lay the meat out so that it is level, and put potatoes, onions and pumpkin, if you like, round the meat, just as you would place vegetables round a roast in a kitchen stove. On to the meat put more hot stones, and more wet leaves over the top of them again. When the leaves entirely cover the stones, and are smouldering, put a big sheet of paper bark over the lot or, failing paper bark, use clean corn sacks or sugar bags, thoroughly wetted. Be sure the sacks have no holes in them, however, because the meat, the stones and the leaves must be absolutely covered.

Now, over everything, throw earth, which must be patted down thoroughly. Look carefully to see that absolutely no smoke can get out of the ground oven.

A piece of beef 3in. thick will be cooked in one hour. The earth is carefully scraped away from the paper bark (or sacks), which must then be picked up slowly at one end and lifted off with the greatest care so that no dirt falls on the food. You will find that the fresh leaves have scented the beef with a delicious flavour which is quite impossible to describe. (Botanists would probably be able to tell you other native Australian trees which have the virtue of imparting a flavour to meat.)

The native people have no way of preserving meat, so they have to deal immediately with any large quantity, such as a whole bullock or dugong.

They leave the skin or hide on and take out all the entrails. Then they make a ground oven big enough to take the whole animal — and a dugong can weigh as much as half a ton. It is quite a sight to see all the women gathered together to make an oven large enough.

Among the aborigines, meat is always distributed according to tribal relationships, so that before it begins to cook each person is free to flavour his or her own piece according to taste.

The grandmother gets the right forequarter, the uncle has the left forequarter, father gets portions of the leg, and so on. It is all strictly according to the law of the tribe. The hunter's right is the head, the meat along the backbone, and the tail.

They have a strange custom which is called "The Vow." The hunter may, by right, ask for a portion of the entrails. He says, "The liver is mine" or "The heart is mine," and that part must be put aside for him. Should anybody eat that portion which the hunter has vowed, he is a breaker of the law.

I knew of a curious instance that illustrates just how seriously the natives regard the breaking of

"The Vow." A native of the Roper River district had contracted leprosy, and when I asked him how he caught it, he told me this story:

"I vowed a piece of liver, and another man ate it. I found out that he had done this, and I sang a magic song which made him vomit up my Vow. When he had vomited it up, I ate it—and this is how I got leprosy."

He had become a very magic man and was held in high respect for what he had done. Nevertheless, he had leprosy.

GRILLING STEAK. Much discussion centres around the cuts of beef to be used for grilling, and the length of time it should be hung after the beast has been killed. Contrary to generally-held ideas, I have seen steak cut from the freshly-killed beast tossed straight on to the coals; it made excellent eating. Neckbone steak and short ribs, however, are the best cuts.

To grill meat in the bush, we make a fire with small sticks, preferably from a gum tree. After the fire has burned down, blow off the white ashes with a green bush or, as in the Northern Territory, with a goose wing. Should the coals be too ashy, we cover them with small green twigs, and on these place the steak. Do not salt it until it is cooked, as salt makes the meat tough. A long thin stick, sharpened at one end, is an excellent fork for turning the steak over.

A delicious addition is to rub the following mixture well into both sides of the steak before grilling:

One teaspoonful each of Chinese soy sauce, tomato sauce and worcestershire sauce, and some grated garlic.

RIB BONES. The long rib bones are very good when cooked on the coals, but the best way to serve them is to cut them into 6in. lengths, coat them with flour and salt, and steam in a casserole with cut-up onions for about $2\frac{1}{2}$ hours.

MILK GUT. This makes a very tasty meal. Cut the milk gut into lengths of 3in. or 4in., and either grill or cook in a dry frying pan. Salt and pepper to taste after cooking.

CORNED BEEF. The bush method of cooking corned beef (preferably the second cut, brisket) is to wash it to take away the salt, then cover with cold water. After bringing it to the boil, cook it until it slides off the prongs of a fork. The beef is cooled in its liquor, which is known as "pot liquor" and can always be used for cooking cabbage, halved potatoes or onions or even — as we have seen — for making damper when the cream of tartar supply runs out.

HOW TO SALT BEEF (bush method). 14lb. of coarse salt to one medium-sized bullock.

Cut the beef into portions up to about 5lb. If the pieces are large, make a few cuts in the thicker parts. Rub the beef thoroughly in salt and leave it to brine on a heap of green bushes. preferably gum. When the salting is finished, the beef is covered for about 24 hours, and at night the bushes are spread out, and the pieces are laid out in the night air. Next morning, the beef is stacked again, and covered well against the flies.*

BUSH GAME (geese, ducks, etc.). Wild ducks and geese, especially the larger varieties, make delicious eating when cooked by bush methods.

* Fish can be cured in the same manner, except that a mixture of half salt and half sugar is required, to keep the flavour.

Some geese are hard to pluck, and there is not always enough hot water to spare for plucking in the usual way. Therefore, the goose is dipped well in cold water, thrown on the fire, and rolled quickly around. The water, of course, begins to steam immediately, and the steam softens the quills. The goose can then be plucked quite easily.

When the bird has been plucked and dressed, it is ready to cook. It is cut right down the middle of the backbone and opened up like a book. If a meal is wanted in a hurry, the opened bird can be grilled like a steak, and it is quite delicious.

To cook the bird in a ground oven, you might try the following method, which has been adopted by white people who have mixed with the Waddaman tribe: Gather lemon grass and soak it in water. When the ground oven is ready, hot stones are put into the wet lemon grass and all is then put inside the split bird. The bird is folded over again, tied up and put on the steaming leaves of the ground oven in the usual way. Vegetables can be put with it, if desired. Cover in the way I have already described, and leave it for about $\frac{3}{4}$ of an hour, or perhaps a little longer, according to the size of the bird. The bird is most delicious to eat, with the lemon flavour inside and gumleaf flavour in the crisp skin.

KANGAROOS. All of the kangaroo is good to eat, but the legs, when cooked and skinned, look not unlike ham, and if you wish to make them really tasty, make incisions in the flesh with a sharp knife and insert small pieces of bacon.

KANGAROO HEAD. The head of a kangaroo, split

open and thoroughly washed, makes an excellent stew with the tail put in as well.

KANGAROO TAIL. The tail of a kangaroo or wallaby can be used as a basis for stew exactly like an oxtail.

BAKED KANGAROO TAIL. First, remove the hair from the skin, which must be left on the tail. After cleaning, cut into pieces the width of the cooking pot. Lay the pieces in the pot with some water, to which a little fat and some salt have been added, and bake in a hot oven. Kangaroo Tail is very good baked in the ashes; and cooked in a ground oven with the hide still on it, it is marvellous. All the sinews jellify, and are lovely to eat.

KANGAROO TAIL SOUP. Roast the tail in the ground oven, or cut it into lengths (as described above) and bake it in the camp oven, having first scraped off the hair. After baking for two to two and a half hours, the skin will come off easily. When the tail has been skinned, cut it into sections and coat it with flour. Put it into the cooking pot with water to cover, pepper and salt, a little butter or a portion of bacon, and cut up potatoes, carrots and onions. Let it simmer for $1\frac{1}{2}$ hours, or until the meat starts to leave the bones.

KANGAROO CASSEROLE. (For 4 people). Take a leg of kangaroo (about 2lb.) and slice the meat into pieces about $\frac{1}{4}$in. thick. Cut three or four potatoes into long slices of the same thickness, also three onions and the same quantity of pumpkin. Butter the bottom of the saucepan and put in a layer of kangaroo meat, then a layer of sliced vegetables, then more butter, more meat, more vegetables, alternately, until the pot is almost filled. Then add a little water,

33

about a quarter way up the pot, put it over a quick fire to bring it to the boil, and let it simmer for about three hours. Do not stir, but make sure there is always a little liquid at the bottom of the pot. The best container for this dish is a tall casserole pot, such as they use in France, but an ordinary saucepan will do.

BANDICOOTS. The bandicoot is cleaned by removing the entrails through an incision in the side, and it is cooked on the coals. The flesh, which is very white and firm, is not unlike rabbit. I knew a missionary's wife on Groote Island who used to buy bandicoots from the natives when she could not get chickens, because she thought bandicoot meat was an excellent food for children.

ROAST STUFFED BANDICOOT. Bandicoot can be scraped like a pig. Clean it, and stuff it with a mixture of dry breadcrumbs, onion, salt, pepper and herbs, and bake it in a hot oven.

BAKED BANDICOOT. Scrape it after first plunging it in water (two parts boiling to one part cold) to soften the hairs. When it is well scraped, even to the head, clean out the mouth and, if it is a male, cut out the gland at the base of the tail. Sprinkle with salt and let it hang for two or three hours, or overnight. Then wash it well and fill it with savoury stuffing (see above), sew up the skin, put the bandicoot in the camp oven with a little fat and water; place the camp oven over hot coals and cover it with hot ashes. Baste it and turn it over from time to time, and let it roast thoroughly.

BANDICOOT SCALLOPS. Cut the bandicoot, scraped and cleaned, into four portions. Boil it in hot salted water until it is nearly cooked. Take it out and let it drain and dry thoroughly at the side of the fire for about 15 minutes. Make a batter of egg yolk, milk and half a spoonful of mustard. Dip each piece into the batter, then coat it in dry breadcrumbs. Fry in boiling fat until it turns golden brown.

POSSUMS. Being gumleaf eaters, possums are cooked by leaving the entrails in. Toss a possum on the fire until cooked, when the shrunken entrails can be easily removed. When the burnt skin is removed, the flesh has a delicate flavour of eucalyptus. This is an acquired taste, but it is very good.

POSSUM PUMPKIN PIE. In the early days, possums were caught, cleaned and cut up, put into a hollowed-out pumpkin which was then roasted until the meat was cooked — a very tasty pie it was, too.

Bandicoots and possums (and flying-foxes, which are dealt with in Chapter Five) can be dressed and treated in the same way as chicken or rabbits.

A very disconcerting shape indeed

4

How to Bake a Snake

How tasty is food when it's cooked in the stones
    In the ways of our fathers of old!
How tasty the flesh, how sweet are the bones!
    So follow this way as it's told.

—B.H.

MOST PEOPLE HAVE an antipathy to snakes, and will not eat them because they do not like to touch them or even look at them. All the same, the flesh is excellent eating, as is the flesh of the goanna.

HOW TO BAKE A SNAKE. If a snake is killed and thrown straight on to the fire, it immediately twists and turns into a very disconcerting shape indeed. To cook it in the approved manner, you need a fire and two people. They sit one each side of the fire and stretch the snake over the heat, passing it to and fro slowly. The idea of this, the natives say, is to throw the juices back into the flesh and at the same time relax the muscular contractions. When it has completely ceased to wriggle and twist, it is laid lengthways on the ground (it is never cut) and with the aid of a sharp knife or a piece of glass bottle or flint, incisions are made right along both sides close to the backbone, about $\frac{1}{4}$in. deep, thus cutting all the sinewy parts. When this is done, the cook bends the snake to make it supple and rolls

37

it up just like a butcher rolls a rib roast. This is tied up with a piece of string, slipped under the hot coals, covered up with ashes and left to cook. When it is tender on one side, it is turned over. It makes quite a shapely roast. It is served after the gut has been removed. The fat is still intact, in delicious round nodules, the flesh is white and firm, and it tastes — well, a little like chicken. (According to the natives it is much better than fowl.)

Water Snakes, which are cooked in practically the same manner, are a real delicacy.

A special delicacy are the eggs from the female snake, which have a very creamy consistency.

GOANNAS. There is an art in cooking goannas. They must always be felt very tenderly by an expert to see that the fat is inside, because on the quantity of fat in a goanna depends its value as a food and as a delicacy. If it has plenty of fat it must not be held up too long by the neck, or the thin membrane holding the fat will break. The secret is to keep the fat in the membrane bag inside the belly.

Before it is cooked, it is placed on the fire and turned over until all the scales become crisp. A native will tell you that this is also intended to drive the juices back into the flesh. The vent is held to the fire to make it tender, then sprinkled with sand, and the entrails are carefully drawn out with an expert twist. When it is clean, another incision is made under the forearm. A little hooked stick is put in and turned round to get the liver and lights out — very gently. The gall bladder is then broken off, and the liver is pushed back.

The reptile is cooked lengthways in the ground oven. The best parts are the ribs and the arms, though — with typical politeness — the natives always give the tail to white men, who imagine it is the best part to eat.

The fat is always taken out and everyone eats some. You can eat up to a teacupful of goanna fat and it will not give you indigestion, and the eggs are excellent. Like most other good, rich food, goanna eggs are taboo to the young — so are crocodile eggs, fat bandicoots and fat turkeys. All these are the prerogative of the old men, who assure the young people that such food would cause them to break out in terrible sores.

A great number of the Aborigines' taboos, of course, are bound up with knowledge that has been handed down over the ages.

A great bush friend of mine called Jimmy Gibbs told me of how, when short of meat in the bush, he and his native stockmen caught a big goanna. After examination, the aborigines pronounced it "unfit to eat." Jimmy, thinking this was just some aboriginal taboo, insisted that it was "good tucker," and cooked and ate it.

"Never again!" Jimmy told me. He became violently ill and they had to carry him on a rough bush stretcher for three days till he reached the homestead and some soft, light foods that slowly brought him round.

Blue-tongues are cooked exactly like goannas. I once asked a native woman who was eating a water hen, what it tasted like. "Like a blue-tongue," she said. "And what does that taste like?" "Like a snake." In other words, it is not possible to describe the flavour of these meats which the Aborigines have eaten for thousands of years, and which I and many other white men find quite delicious. They have their own special flavour, just like beef, mutton or chicken.

I have many times been asked what dugong tastes like. The answer, of course, is that it tastes like — dugong.

It is thought that the dugong, or sea-cow (related to the manatee) started the myths of mermaids which were taken back to Europe by the voyaging sailors of the old days. It is a sea-water mammal like the whale. The females suckle their young, held between the flippers, and as they surface, they make a noise which sounds for all the world like a heavy human sigh. Seeing these round-headed creatures with young ones in their arms, sighing in such a human fashion, no doubt the superstitious sailors thought them to be women of the sea.

Dugong makes very good eating indeed. As I have said elsewhere, they are enormous creatures weighing up to half a ton, so the cooking of a dugong is quite an undertaking. The native women scoop out a ground oven and set a fire in it. After the fire has burned down and the stones are red hot, the women arrange the stones evenly, using pieces of bark shaped rather like badminton bats. They have to cover an area about 6ft. x 4ft. The dugong. suitably flavoured, is placed on these stones, then covered with another layer of stones, paper bark, and finally with sand to seal off all the steam. The mound is about 2ft. 6in. high.

It is left to cook all day, and in the night, just as the sun goes down, all the people come round, scrape the sand off carefully, and peel off the paper bark, which is left on the ground in large pieces to serve as plates. Then the meat is put out, according to the law of tribal distribution.

Naturally, as the old men of the tribe have got to look after themselves (for the Aborigines have no Old Age Pension Schemes or anything of that sort), they keep to an ancient custom, a form of magic, which guarantees that they will have plenty of dugong meat for themselves. Once the first feast is over, the elders throw the meat into a taboo known as "goodoo-goodoo," and none of the young people are permitted to eat any more. If they do, the elders tell them, it will turn into poison and kill them.

The meat under the "goodoo-goodoo" taboo is put on top of a rough platform so that the dogs — there are always dogs in a native camp — cannot reach it, and the ground right round the platform is cleared and carefully brushed in accordance with the taboo.

As the young fellows cannot eat any more of it, they have to go out and kill another dugong, so off they go again to the estuaries. By the time they get back, the old men have eaten the remainder of the taboo meat, and once more there is plenty of fresh dugong to eat.

Naturally, all the dugong will not be eaten in a single day, but there will be quite a lot of "goodoo-goodoo" meat which is underdone after the first cooking. The women remake the fire next day and cook the meat again. By continual cooking it lasts for several days, and, strangely enough, cooked by this method, the flavour and quality of the meat remain unaffected.

This seems to be a suitable place for commenting on the idea of the ground oven. Centuries ago, our ancestors cooked their beasts by turning them on a spit, and everyone who has eaten meat cooked on the spit knows that it is very good. Nevertheless, during the process of cooking the skinned beast, the fat and juices run and drip into the fire, and are quite lost. The ground oven method has the great virtue of holding in every scrap of fat, juice and flavour. Admittedly it is primitive, and perhaps the city housewife would think several times before she consented to cook in a ground oven rather than in her own gas or electric stove. However, it is still true that our white man's methods are such as to cause the loss of much goodness. The great chefs devised most elaborate methods to retain the juices and flavour of meat — an achievement which the natives of Australia mastered long ago in their simple ground oven.

No one would willingly eat a roast of meat which had been re-cooked several times in a gas oven, it would be absolutely dry and tasteless. Dugong, re-cooked in the ground oven, remains tasty and juicy.

I am told that in America, people are having a craze for cooking on hot stones. Here we are in a country where the method has been used for thousands of years. Perhaps some resourceful person will be able to persuade white Australians to try ground oven cooking. The late Walter Magnus, a great

Sydney chef and gourmet, was very lyrical over the cooking in Tahiti, where they use a somewhat similar method to the Aborigines of Australia, and no one would question his ability to tell good food from bad.

Many city people have barbecues in their gardens these days. It is also quite possible to have a ground oven in the garden, provided you can find a spot of hard clayey earth. All that is needed is to dig a hole about 18in. long, 9in. deep and 12in. wide. When it is needed, light a fire in it, and when the fire has died down, shovel out the ashes, leaving some on the bottom, put heated stones on the remaining ash, then moist leaves. Now put in whatever it is desired to cook; now cover the hole with a piece of flat galvanised iron, make the edges airtight, shovel hot coals or stones on this covering, and leave the food to cook.

Even stranger beasts . . .

5

Even Stranger Beasts

*When we're sitting in the orchard in the cool of
    summer eves,*

*And we hear them blasted flying foxes up among
    the leaves,*

*My old bush mate says, "Crikey!", and he rushes
    for a stick;*

*"Them foxes is good tucker, pal, let's cook 'em
    flamin' quick!"*

—B.H.

EVERYONE KNOWS ABOUT Wichetty Grubs. They are
quite common throughout Australia, and you may
have discovered them in the trees of your garden.

There seems to be an idea that Wichetty Grubs
are revolting to eat, but really, as many people will
tell you, they are excellent. They can be eaten raw,
but in my opinion they are nicer cooked.

When cooked on the clean white ashes of a wood
fire, they are crisp, with a very nice flavour which
is difficult to describe, but which perhaps is just
a little like egg. All you have to do is just cut them
out from the trees and cook them over the coals,
or in a frying pan with a dab of butter to give them
an extra flavour.

I venture to say that if Wichetty Grubs had been

found in abundance in England, so that the poor people could have cooked them, they would today be considered a great delicacy everywhere, like the large white snails and the frogs of France, or Russian caviar.

Food is largely a matter of our circumstances. For instance, in ancient Peru and Mexico, iguanas were a great delicacy relished by the kings, whereas in Australia goannas are scorned — possibly because the Aborigines eat them.

If no one had ever seen an oyster before the white men came to Australia, how many people would eat them? Meanwhile, let me recommend Grilled Wichetty Grubs. You may be pleasantly surprised to find what good tucker they are.

FLYING FOXES

In every country in the world where flying foxes (fruit bats) appear in great numbers, the native peoples of the region consider them a national delicacy, that is, in every country except Australia! Only people who have never seen them in abundance in their own native lands, and who have plenty of other foods, look upon these little creatures with disgust.

In New Guinea and among the Aborigines, some of the methods of hunting them are very ingenious, a fact which proves that they are much sought after as food.

There is a strange objection to flying foxes; it is said that they have a horrible smell. Yet I have often been with white people when the natives have brought in flying foxes, and have asked them to smell the creatures. They have always been amazed to find no more than the ordinary smell of any other wild creature.

This mistaken idea arises from the fact that the big rookeries where they sleep do have a strong odour, something similar, as a matter of fact, to a fowl house. But we do not object to eating fowls — or pigs — because of the smell of their runs.

I am reminded of an incident I witnessed once. Some missionaries and their wives were sitting under a tree eating chicken. Not far away, some native women were enjoying a meal of flying foxes. The missionaries watched them for a while, and one said: "I don't know how they can eat those disgusting creatures." I strolled over to the native women. Nibbling their flying foxes, they looked over at the missionaries and shook their heads. "How come they eat dirty fowls?" they said. "Fowls pick up all dirty food round the yard. Not good tucker."

It's a matter of what you are accustomed to!

Three or four flying foxes make a very good meal. As a bush mate once said to me, "If I had my way, I would compel every man by law to eat flying foxes to repletion at least once a year." You saturate yourself with chlorophyll when you eat them, as they themselves eat nothing but honey, the nectar of flowers and ripe, wholesome fruit.

Flying fox is a food *par excellence*. There is no preparation needed. You just throw them on the coals or on to a big fire, burn the wings and cut the membrane off near the body. When the fire has burned down to smouldering coals, put the little foxes on the coals, cover them with more hot coals, and cook them, entrails and all.

When cooked, they are taken out with a long stick and tossed on some waiting branches to cool off. When I was in the boat trading in the Gulf of Carpentaria, we would cook as many as 200 or 300 at a time. They last for quite a while; we knew they would keep us going for four or five days, because owing to the way they are cooked, they are sealed up inside the outer skin.

To eat a flying fox, you need the book of bush etiquette. Hold it with the chest facing away from you and the backbone close to you, gripping it in your two hands with your thumbs along the backbone. You press with the thumbs and the flesh on both sides of the backbone breaks. in. Then you bring the thumbs over, and that loosens the flesh right off the ribs. Then get him by the neck and pull the body completely free of all the flesh. Thus, the whole casket of the chest case, entrails and head are put down beside you on the plate. You then delicately pick the meat off the skin. The little legs are just like ham, surrounded by a coating of fat. The heart is also surrounded by fat. Every part of the flying fox can be eaten, except the gall bladder. Even the bones are soft and edible.

MALAYAN METHOD. The Malays cook flying foxes in the oven and then shred the meat into a big bowl. They make a sauce of soy, ginger, etc., and this is put into another bowl. Everyone gathers round, dips a piece of flying fox into the sauce, and eats it.

A Malayan friend of mine in Darwin had a lot of mango trees. When the fruit was full of foxes, and he had shot as many of the little creatures as he wanted, he would send me a message: "Come down today, and we will have a feast."

The native method of cooking them preserves all the goodness inside the skin. The Malayan method adds the tasty flavourings of the East. Flying foxes can also be dressed and roasted like chickens, and the flesh would indeed lend itself to any of the usual approved ways of cooking chickens. I believe that a year or two ago, some Sydney suburbs were visited by a plague of flying foxes, driven further south than usual. I wonder how many of the householders, fixing nets over their fruit trees, realised that they were entertaining one of the most delicious animals in the Southern Hemisphere?

When the natives want to catch flying foxes, they go to the rookeries, being careful to rub themselves with mud so that the foxes will not catch the scent of human beings. They affix pieces of paper bark to long sticks. The bark has previously been well beaten so that it will burn quickly, and when it is lighted, it is held up in the air towards the foxes, hanging head downwards. The smoke confuses them, the torches burn them, and they drop to the ground.

In New Guinea, big nets are stretched across the valleys to entangle the little foxes as they come flying through.

To the native, everything is food. If you can't eat it, it isn't food; if you can, it is. Food is divided into two categories, light and heavy. Heavy food is that which sticks to your ribs and keeps you going.

Before recoiling in horror at the idea of eating Wichetty Grubs and Flying Foxes, not to mention Snakes and Goannas, it is salutary to remember that many men who went to the war would have been shocked at the idea of eating cats and dogs, yet, as

49

prisoners of war, they ate them and found them not too bad. Food, at the start, is a matter of necessity. It is only custom which turns certain foods into a delicacy, and sometimes sentiment which makes other foods taboo. I remember, in France, seeing horses' carcasses hanging up for sale for human consumption. Horse meat is very good, and furthermore the horse is not subject to certain diseases which attack cattle. But we revere the horse and do not eat him, and when the people of Chicago found recently that they had been sold hamburgers containing a percentage of ground horse meat, there was almost a riot.

Oddly enough, horse meat is freely sold for the use of pet dogs and cats. Human customs are indeed strange and various.

Whistling steak

6

Aboriginal Wisdom

To make food go further
Eat less.

—Aboriginal saying.

THE NATIVES, WITHOUT benefit of modern science, found out long ago many things regarding food values. Some, perhaps, would say that their instinct guided them to what is good food.

Everyone knows that the Australian Aborigines have never been a crop-growing people. How was it, then, that they never contracted vitamin-deficiency diseases before the white man came?

One food that they found to be not only edible but extremely nutritive was the Nymphacea Lily. Every bit of this water plant can be eaten.*

The tuber, a large yellow potato-like growth at the base of the plant, is cooked on the coals of the fire. It is rather unusual in flavour — another acquired taste — but it is a good and nourishing vegetable. The natives also eat the seed pods, but they are careful to see that their young children do not get hold of them, as the pods are difficult to digest. The method of treating these seed pods is to grind them between stones, or on a board with a rolling pin, and when ground up they become the basis

* For some recipes, see Chapter Nine.

for quite a number of things, being used instead of flour. They can be mixed with flour and eaten like a cake.

To overcome the indigestibility of these pods, the native mothers first chew the cooked or raw seed pod cake, and then feed this predigested meal to young children who in time are able to eat it themselves without any ill effect.

Arising from this custom is a strange form of eating among the aborigines of Melville and Bathurst Islands. It is called "Buninginni." Living for some time among these people, I noticed that they would regurgitate some food after a large meal and begin chewing as would a cud-chewing animal. They explained that this was a common custom in the past. They were taught to do it by their parents, who claimed that it was good for their digestion. To me it seemed a strange and ugly practice, but to them it was part of the daily meal. Another habit of these people is to cook large quantities of a special white earth that forms the cliffs of these islands, and eat it as one eats a meal.

But to return to the Lily: The big stalks that grow in every pond can be eaten raw or cut up and eaten in a white sauce like any other vegetable. The tender ends are chopped up and boiled in a little water, and the sauce is simply made with milk and flour. They are very essential as green vegetables. Many a time I have seen the native people coming in from dry areas with their breast-fed babies, and the mothers with hardly sufficient milk to keep the infants alive. After three or four days at the big lily lagoons, the women's breasts would be full of milk again, and the babies would start to thrive.

Quite a few bushmen have, by living on native foods, lived to a great age and kept good health. Many of them consistently ate the wild honey sugar bags of the bush, mixed with bee bread, and this not only kept them healthy but acted as a mild aperient. On the other hand, people who were too "delicate" to eat black-fella tucker often became seriously ill from vitamin deficiencies, on a constant diet of salt beef and damper with black tea and sugar. This was in the days when all food was carried from distant markets by horse or camel teams. Now, air services have changed all that.

Much of the history of the outback can be read in the scourges of vitamin-deficiency diseases which swept the country. One sickness, in 1915, struck the Georgina River country in West Queensland, and quite a few people died of a form of beri-beri which, they said, was caused by bad flour from the Argentine. It was, of course, nothing of the sort.

It was remarkable to see the way some of the bushmen persisted in eating only their own food when all around them the natives were gathering fresh food from the bush. One man, named Brooks, at the Carlo Border Netting Camp near the Mulligan River, was smitten with the vitamin deficiency disease which carried people off so quickly. Realising that he was going to die, he asked the natives to dig a grave in a sandy patch under a shady tree. When the grave was dug, with bushes and a blanket laid on the bottom of the hole, he lay down in it and wrote a letter to the nearest boundary rider, 25 miles away; he wrote that he was dying, and asked his mate to come up and look after his things. He explained that he had got the natives to dig his grave so that he would not make a nuisance of himself to others. He sent his letter off by a foot-walk native, and when the other rider galloped up, he was dead, lying in his grave under the tree.

It is strange and sad to think of him dying so bravely, in his lonely grave, when all around him were wild yams, anyeroo nuts growing prolifically in the sandhills, and the various wild bananas and nuts of the region.

This melancholy little tale illustrates the fact that it is always advisable to know the trees that are around you, to know the types of food that can be got from the trees.

For instance, the common Fan Palm (Livingstonia) is an intensely valuable article of diet. The cabbage-like inner part at the crown of the tree is an excellent food, and is eaten by the natives of the Northern Territory.

It was Leichhardt who first showed that an excellent coffee substitute can be made from Kurrajong seed pods, roasted and ground in the same way as coffee. He drank it all the time he was on his trip, but very few people think of using it today. The flavour is amazingly like coffee, though it makes a rather weaker brew.

A similar illustration is the way we people eat both English and sweet potatoes, which were first introduced to us by native peoples of other countries, and turn up our noses at the native Australian potatoes, dismissing them as "yams" — forgetting that the word "potato" is simply the American Indian word for their own "yams." Yet the big Rockas and Murungas of the North are in the same family as "potatoes"; they are best when baked in the coals. Like the Taro and other wild potatoes, they tend to turn blue if they are boiled.

Only the experts know the good wild potatoes from the bad. I have learned from the natives their tried and proven methods of testing, but still, great care needs to be taken by the inexperienced bush-man.

One of the native methods is to drive a finger-nail into the freshly-dug tuber, and hold the nail at a certain angle to the sun. If a dull light is reflected from the drying yam-juice on the nail, then the tuber is "cheeky" (poisonous). If, however, the nail shows no reflected light, then it is edible.

The same test is occasionally applied by breaking the tuber in half and holding the broken surfaces to the light.

Wild honey is a staple food of the Aboriginal diet, but they always see that it is thoroughly mixed with bee-bread, which turns it creamy. When honey is eaten raw, it is best to do as the natives do: Mix it with certain edible grasses. They suck the honey out of the grass, so that the saliva mixes sufficiently with the honey to make it digest easily in the stomach.

Honey plays an important part in Aboriginal ritual. As most people know, the Aborigines do not believe that the father plays any part at all in the conception of the child. After elaborate ceremonies, in accordance with the ancient beliefs of these people, a young woman is judged pregnant — that is, a spirit child has passed into her womb. It is then the father's duty to give her some wild honey to eat.

They believe that the spirit child will like the taste of the honey and will stay happily where he (or she) is.

Even now that they are in constant touch with the whites, the natives often keep healthier than their masters. The offal of the killing yards is the portion of the Aboriginal workers on any station, while the choicer cuts are set aside for the white men. This does not always turn out quite as intended. In the time of the big beri-beri scourge which I have already mentioned, which spread right across the Northern Territory, I remember that Dr Cook, who was then the Chief Protector of the Aborigines and also chief medical man, mentioned the absence of beri-beri among the native population. He said it was due to the fact that they ate their tripe without going to too much trouble about cleaning it. The pre-digested grass in the tripe acted as a vegetable and kept them healthy, whereas the white men, who had no vegetables and ate only the choicer cuts of meat, were smitten with beri-beri through lack of vitamin C.

The native method of preparing tripe is severely simple. The women collect it from the killing yards, slash it across and beat it against a convenient post to knock the grass, etc., out of it. When this is done, the tripe is taken to the nearby waterhole and washed. Then it is cooked in the ground oven. When it is cooked, the inner membrane can be skinned off quite easily, leaving the pure white flesh. Tripe is considered by the native people to be a great delicacy. They do not at all appreciate the white man's habit of stewing tripe: They reckon that stewed tripe has not got the real flavour about it.

THE WHISTLING STEAK. A fact discovered by the aborigines, and useful to people who are hard-pressed for food, is that food soaked in water loses any poisonous content (as witness the treatment of cycad palm nuts). Anything that has "gone off" is soaked by the Aborigines.

I remember a 10lb. piece of rump steak that was hanging so long that it swelled up and went perfectly green. In fact, it whistled when you passed it. I yelled out to one of the native people to throw it away. He said, "No, we'll take it to the camp and eat it. This is good tucker."

This is what the natives did: They soaked that piece of steak for two days in running water, then they cooked it in the ground oven with leaves around it, as usual, to flavour it. After it was cooked and taken out, it looked so beautiful and smelled so good that I reckoned I would have a little bit of it. It was absolutely marvellous! It was tender and tasty, and provided that you could get over the fact that it had been green, it made a fine meal.

A veterinary friend later told me that it was quite safe to have eaten the "whistling steak." The bacilli that poisons people, he said, are only on the meat when it *first* starts to go off. Once meat goes green *it is not poisonous*. The water and the fire destroyed both the bacilli and the smell.

The bush people, when beef goes slightly "off," pour some vinegar into a bowl of water and wash the meat. This takes away the taint. Condy's crystals, also, take away the unpleasant smell.

I remember a time when a certain bush cook was boiling some mutton. Just before the men were due to come in for the meal, he discovered that one of the pieces of meat in the pot was slightly tainted. He whipped it out, but the smell had spread to the rest of the mutton. What to do? There was no time to start cooking all over again, nor, for that matter, did he have any more meat ready.

Hurriedly, he cut up plenty of onions, put them to cook in a little hot water, thickened it with flour and milk and added plenty of salt and pepper. He served the mutton with a tasty onion sauce which disguised the unfortunate flavour, the men pronounced the stew to be excellent, and naturally no one suffered any harm from the meal.

Modern methods of food preservation are not always available in the bush, so this cook was only doing what his ancestors had to do in Europe before the days of refrigeration — disguising the taste of stale meat with a fine sauce. Of course, spices and strongly flavoured sauces, now valued for their own sakes, date from the old days when cooks had to learn to overcome the repulsive smell of stale meat! When Venice "held the gorgeous East in fee," she was the centre of the spice trade. The merchants knew that their customers would pay large sums for spices to put with meat. Nowadays, city and country people spend the money on refrigerators instead. But sometimes, in the bush, we have to revert to the old ways . . .

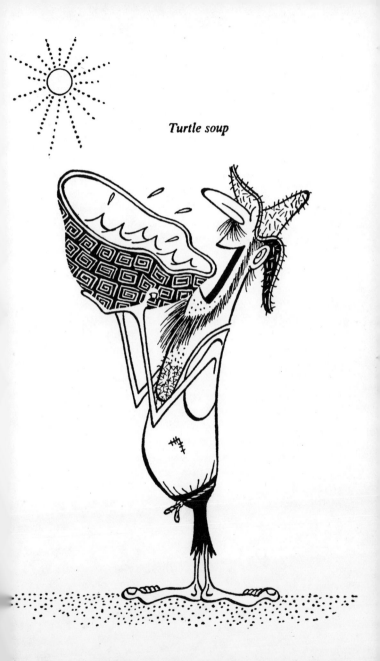

Turtle soup

7

Turtles

Come all you city slickers now and join me on the
*   beach,*
There's turtle soup and turtle steaks all well within
*   your reach,*
We'll heat the stones and spread the sacks beside
*   the big lagoon*
And feast like fighting cocks, we will, by the light
*   of the golden moon.*

—B.H.

TURTLES ARE SUPREMELY good tucker. The Aborigines in the coastal regions think very highly of turtle meat, turtle fat, turtle eggs and the delicious juices which make a fine turtle broth. Like bush turkeys, turtles are now protected in the regions of the Barrier Reef, but we are still able to obtain them in the Territory, and, believe me, a turtle feast is something you don't forget.

The method of cooking turtles on Melville Island is this: The natives generally watch the beaches, and capture the turtles as they come up to lay their eggs. The captured creature is first turned over on its back and killed. Next, they make a hole at the base of the neck and through this hole remove all the entrails, including the liver and the heart. The gullet is cleaned and turned inside out, and carefully set aside, as also is the long, cleaned gut.

A big fire is blazing away, as I described in the chapter on cooking dugongs. As it burns down, the cooks grill their special "perks" — the liver and smaller pieces of the edible organs. Then the main cooking begins. The eggs that are still left inside the turtle — that is, the soft eggs — are taken out and stuffed into the prepared gullet, which swells to the size of a pineapple. If there are any eggs left over, they are put into the gut to form a large sausage that may be anything up to 2ft. long.

An interesting point is that two features in these cooking preparations bear some resemblance to the cooking of the ancient Greeks and Romans. Firstly, the Aboriginal method of taking out the gut from the base of the neck or, as in the case of goannas and bandicoots, below the shoulder, is the same method as the ancients used in gutting pigs.

Secondly, the belly of a hen containing soft eggs was part of the ingredients used by the Greeks for stuffing meat puddings.

I have mentioned before that the native people of Australia consider the soft eggs of the snake a great delicacy, as they do the soft eggs of the female turtle. I mention these things to show that though our cooking methods have changed in recent centuries, the fathers of our civilisation — the Greeks — shared many cooking customs with the Australian Aborigines.

To get back to our turtle. When the fire has burned down, it is time to start cooking the turtle, which has been thoroughly washed and cleansed with salt water. Hot stones are now put into the cavity from which the entrails have been removed, then the turtle is laid on its back in the coals and more hot stones and coals are laid upon it. The opening at the neck is made steam-proof with leaves well rammed home. The whole is covered in the usual way and left to cook. Meanwhile, the gullet and the sausage are put into hot sand or hot ashes, and inside an hour or two, when the eggs are hard-cooked, they are taken out and laid aside to cool. These egg sausages, which last for several days, are eaten in slices — and very good they are, too.

After three or four hours, the ashes are scraped off the turtle; a knife is used to cut round the carapace of the belly, which is torn off and put aside; the stones are removed, and the cooked flesh is exposed. All the stones that were inside are carefully removed, and the shell now looks like a great inverted bowl, only the legs and arms remain to adhere to the sides. In the bottom of the shell are all the juices that have run out during the cooking. Now salt and pepper are added to the steaming broth, and everyone present dips in his pannikin for a taste of the first course.

After the soup comes the meat. The green turtle fat is solid, like beef fat, and in the eating a piece of flesh is wrapped round a smaller bit of green fat. If you are still hungry, you can have a slice of turtle egg sausage later on, as a savoury.

Freshwater turtles (known as "Long Neck" turtles) are caught in the swamps where they lie during the dry months of the year under the hard ground, awaiting the rain. The native people find a Long Neck by spotting the air holes and then digging down with a sharp rod of iron or wood. When they hit the turtle under the hard mud, they can feel its breathing through the impact of the stick, and they dig it out and carry it back to camp. It is cooked in the same way as saltwater turtle.

Turtle meat, after it has been cooked in the oven, can be cut into little cubes, put into the frying pan and cooked as a curry, but *it must always be baked in the ground oven first*. The cook melts turtle fat in the pan, adds chopped onions and curry powder, and cooks the meat in the pan until it becomes crisp. Then he thickens the curry with a little flour, adds some water — and this is a fine Malayan Dry Curry, made with delicious turtle meat and cooked in fresh turtle fat.

In other places, the sea turtle is cut up before it is cooked — of course, it is sealed over the hot fire to drive the juices into the flesh, according to native custom, before it is cut up. Then it is cooked in the stones, the carapace being used to cover the meat instead of paper bark. For this method of cooking, turtle beef is flavoured with gum leaves or grevillea, and potatoes and onions are cooked alongside it.

Sometimes, in the Gulf Country, the natives, instead of putting the cooked sea turtle on bushes, simply put it on the sand. Naturally the beef gets covered with sand, and it is quite a sight to see the old men, sitting down to discuss some topical point, tearing a piece of flesh off the cooked turtle and tapping it with their fingers to emphasise a point. A stream of sand showers down from the meat. Through this custom of eating sandy meat, the teeth of these people get ground down, and it is not uncommon to see a mouthful of absolutely sound teeth, without any decay at all, ground almost down to the gums.

I have already described how unlaid turtle eggs are made into a sausage. Now, should large quantities of laid eggs be discovered, these can be broken into a real paperbark dish, which is then wrapped up, tied with bush string, and baked on the coals of the fire. The result is like a large cake of hard-boiled eggs which will last for several days and is a good stand-by in an emergency. Any eggs can be baked in the ashes, but care must be taken that they are only cooked on the soft white ashes, and that a hole is driven into the upper end of the egg. The eggs are stood up around the fire so that they will cook in the ordinary way, but if there is no hole pierced in the top, you may have an explosion.

TURTLE EGG OMELETTE. Take 12 turtle eggs (there are usually 60 in a nest), wash them well to remove the sand, then break into a dish. Add half a pint of milk, pepper, salt, and any flavouring you require, such as chopped bacon, cheese or herbs. Beat again for two or three minutes. Put a little butter in the frying pan, and when it is smoking hot, pour in the egg mixture, stirring it continuously with a fork or an egg slice. At first it will be very watery, like custard, but with continuous stirring it becomes crisp. Turn it over and over for about 15 minutes. This is a really beautiful dish.

TURTLE EGG GRIDDLE CAKES. Take up to 12 eggs and add four spoonfuls of flour, and a little cream of tartar and baking soda. Beat up well, add a little water, and make it a fairly thick batter.

Pour some batter into a hot greased frying pan, to a thickness of about $\frac{1}{4}$in. It will immediately double or treble in thickness. When it is perfectly brown on the underside, add a little more batter and turn it over to brown on the other side. Turn the griddle cakes on to a hot plate and sprinkle with sugar.

TURTLE SOUP. (Sea-going turtles.) Take the fore-flippers and, after washing them thoroughly, boil them, skin and all, in half a kerosene tin of water, keeping the water constantly up to this level. After a time the skin becomes separated, and can be pulled off the flesh. When this occurs, keep the dish simmering until the whole thing becomes like a jelly. Add some salt. This makes a perfect stock, a basis for turtle soup. All you do to complete the cooking is to add vegetables and flavourings as desired, and finish off.

Sometimes, men in the bush find themselves on a waterless beach, but the knowledgeable ones simply set about looking for nests of turtle eggs. It is bush lore that eggs which are a few weeks old contain fresh water to sustain the young inside. So the bushman breaks the eggs and drinks the water — and saves his life.

And whilst we are on the subject of sea-turtles, I well remember — many years ago — the nights of horror I spent as a guest on the pearling luggers, when the Malayan crew had caught a turtle. As they could not keep the flesh once the creature was killed and cut up, these experts of the "death with a thousand cuts" would simply cut off slices from the living creature in such a manner that it would stay alive for days.

The captain and the crew thought this practice was quite normal, but to hear the creature flapping on deck at night was an experience which still gives me a shudder when I recall it today.

Sea foods

8

More Sea Foods

Fair Australia, oh what a dump.
All you get to eat is crocodile's rump,
Bandicoot's brains and catfish pie.
Let me go home again before I die!

—Old Bush Ballad

I HAVE OFTEN heard described a method of cooking fish by which it is placed in the fire completely smeared with mud, which bakes hard, opens out into two neat plates leaving the fish clean of its skin and scales, and so on. This is something that I have never seen, nor do I know anyone else who has ever seen it. It has never been done in the North. Possibly the now extinct Aboriginal tribes in the South used this method; this would account for the persistent tradition.

This method is also said to be wonderful for duck and other wild game—rendering unnecessary the usual labour of plucking. However, we have never seen birds cooked this way in the Territory, either. I believe that the European gipsy cooked fish by this method.

CRABS. We always insist that crabs, when they are brought in, should be alive and walking about, with the two big nippers intact. Once a crab dies, its flesh putrefies very quickly, and becomes very poisonous. We cook crabs according to the usual practice — boiling them in water — but they are far more delicious cooked on the coals, so that the water inside the crab acts as a boiling medium and turns the meat into very crisp, dry flesh.

Fish do not putrefy so rapidly. The Chinese in the North, and I myself, have eaten fish when it has become quite soft. It is still edible, and quite a number of people prefer it this way.

Fish are cooked by being forced under the coals or into the ashes of the fire, tail first. Certain fish such as mullet must be gutted before they are cooked; the natives slit them along the side like a goanna, so that the ashes cannot go into the flesh. Other fish, that are only grass eaters, can be cooked intact. The gut is more easily removed after it has been cooked.

The Chinese in Darwin say that if you cook a fish in dripping, the fat penetrates through the layers of flesh and causes the fish to become rancid very quickly. They cook fish in boiling peanut oil which, they say, closes up the flesh, so that the fish remains fresh for several days.

FEATHER-TAILED CATFISH. These are freshwater fish, found in the billabongs. They are cleaned out through the mouth, and the fat and air sac are put aside. The fat is now carefully put into the air sac, which is tied, and replaced inside the fish. The gullet is then stuffed with a bit of grass or bush, and the fish is cooked under the ashes of the fire. It is then cleaned of ashes, split open, and the sac of fat is broken over the flesh. This gives the fish a great flavour.

STINGRAYS. The stringray, when caught, is at once cut open so that the condition of the liver can be inspected. If the liver is brownish, it is poor in oil, and the whole fish is thrown away. If the liver is of a creamy consistency, then it is just right for eating.

The whole liver is removed and put aside. The stingray is cleaned and turned on the ashes of the fire, and well cooked on both sides. The flesh is then scraped off and put in a large billy or on a piece of paperbark. Then it is washed in fresh water to soak out the milky juices. When perfectly clean and white, like well-washed clothes, it is formed into balls, one for each person at the feast, and the liver is cut into the same number of pieces. A slight dent is made in each ball, and the piece of liver is placed there. Should you prefer it, you can add a little salt and pepper and eat the liver raw — it is very tasty. But if you like it cooked, take a hot firestick and pass it over the liver (just as a French chef will brown the top of a creme brulee under a "salamander".) The firestick heats the liver and the fat runs a little into the flesh. Under no circumstances should the liver be subjected to hot fire because that destroys the richness and the food value of the liver oil.

The same method of cooking may be used for the baby gummy sharks who inhabit the shallow reaches of the sea. They have a red belly, and the navel is between their fins. They taste excellent if they are cooked like stingray.

Another way of cooking both stingray and gummy shark is as follows:

STINGRAY PIE. After the flesh has been cooked and

washed, put a layer of the flesh on several thicknesses of greased paper. Spread the liver evenly over the flesh, add salt and pepper, and put the rest of the flesh over the liver. Wrap it all up so that it is absolutely flat, in stout paper, and put it into the warm ashes of the fire. It is hot and ready to eat in about 30 minutes. It can be put into a greased piedish, of course, and baked in a very moderate oven for the same length of time. The piedish must be covered, so that the top layer of fish does not dry out.

Most of the food value, of course, lies in the liver, which is heavily impregnated with fat. Strangely enough, you may eat quite freely of this fat without any feeling of biliousness such as you might get from eating beef fat.

CROCODILE EGGS. These are very good eating. They are about the same size as a big goose egg. They can be eaten boiled, when they have a lovely creamy consistency, or they can be roasted in warm ashes, set up on their ends with a hole punched in the top.

Like all other foods that are full of nutriment and delicate in flavour, crocodile eggs are the prerogative of the old men of the tribe, and taboo to the young natives. I knew of one Aboriginal boy who ate crocodile eggs in secret, against the wishes of the elders. His crime was discovered when one of the old men found his track where he had cooked the taboo food. They said nothing, as usual, but shortly afterwards, the lad was mauled by a crocodile. As soon as this happened, the old men pointed out that it served him right, because he had disobeyed the tribal law and had only got the treatment he deserved.

TWO-FELLER CREEK HOTEL

～～～MENU～～～

APPETIZER · PÂTÉ de FOIE STINGRAY.

SOUP · TURTLE, LADLED FROM
GREENBACK SHELL.

ENTREE · WITCHETTY GRUBS AU NATUREL
WITCHETTY GRUBS KEBAB.
BAKED GOANNA EGGS.

DINNER · ROAST FLYING FOX.
HAUNCH OF STUFFED
KANGAROO LEG.

DESSERT · HONEY ANTS.
MULGA NUT KAKES.
MULGA APPLES.

VIN DU PAYS.

9

Life at Durramunkamunni.

"Corn beef and damper, sure we'll have enough,
We'll boil in the bucket such a whopper of a duff!
And as for fish, we'll catch 'em very soon, very soon,
For we'll bait for barramundi on the banks of a
lagoon!"

—Old Bush Ballad.

LAST TIME I was in Sydney, a woman asked me, "Mr. Harney, do you ever eat any bush food?"

"Oh yes," I answered.

"And what do you eat?"

"Well," I said, "I eat eggs, ducks, geese, oysters, fish, mussels, crab—you soon get used to Aboriginal tucker."

She gasped. "I thought they only ate wichetty grubs and raw meat!"

I have tried, in the preceding pages, to dispel this illusion. The natives are only human, after all, and they eat the best food they can get, just as white men do. Though most of their cooking methods are a bit rough according to our ideas, most of them could be adapted very easily to our more hygienic standards. One thing is very certain. The Aborigines know how to get the best out of the foods which are indigenous to Australia—which is more than can be said of almost all white Australians.

Whether you are white or native, you do not need much money to live well alongside the tropical beaches near Darwin. When I lived at Durramunkamunni, the only supplies I had to buy from the store were tea, sugar, milk, flour, some currants and sultanas to make a fruit loaf, and slices of bacon for an omelette. I made my own yeast bread.

This would be a typical day's menu:

Breakfast—Turtle egg omelette, toast and tea.

Dinner—Wild goose or duck, with papaw for vegetable, and a banana from the garden for dessert.

Supper—Grilled fish, and possibly one or two freshly-caught baked crabs.

On the beaches of the North grow plenty of papaws, mangoes and pineapples. There are ample supplies of fish, shellfish and crabs in the sea, turtles and turtle eggs on the beaches, and wild ducks and geese in the bush. I am sure I would not live as well in a city for five times the amount of money I needed at Durramunkamunni.

My mate, Jack Murray, and I would often watch a seagoing turtle crawl up out of the sea and along the beach. After scratching a large hole in the sand, it lays its eggs, usually sixty of them. This creature does not take the slightest notice of human beings, who can walk around it and talk about it, and it goes on with its work quite fearlessly. When it had gone back into the sea, we gathered up the eggs and took them home. I put a dab of butter into the frying pan, cut up a small onion and browned it in the butter, then added turtle eggs — as many as we could eat — with milk and seasoning, and served up a magnificently fresh omelette for breakfast.

Here are some of my favourite recipes from Durramunkamunni:

CURRIED MANGO PICKLE. Take half-ripe mangoes,
skin them, and place them in a big bowl, sliced.
Sprinkle thoroughly with salt, and turn the slices
over from time to time. When thoroughly brined,
grind up some ginger and add it to some curry
powder and well-chopped chillies. Next, drain the
mango thoroughly, sprinkle the ginger and other
ingredients over, and rub well in. When all the
mango slices are thoroughly covered with the mixture, put into a glass jar, stop it up thoroughly and
leave. This is a lovely pickle to serve with cold meat.

CURRIED GOOSE. Slice two or three geese in half
along the backbone, salt them and let them stand.
Get a large casserole or camp oven, put it on the stove
and in this melt some butter (or preferably some
goose fat). Cut up three onions, add them, and when
they are turning brown add curry powder to taste,
according to whether you like a curry to be very hot
or just medium. When the perfume rises from the
curry, add two pints of water and into the liquid put
the halved geese. Cook slowly for $1\frac{1}{2}$ to 2 hours,
then add a good handful of raisins and two big spoonfuls of lime-juice. Let the curry cool slightly, skim
off all the fat, thicken with a little flour and put back
on the stove. Cook for another half hour, and it is
ready to serve.

FRIED PAPAW. Take a half-ripe papaw, slice into
thicknesses of about one-third of an inch, and take
out the seeds. Put some butter into a pan, and when
it is smoking, fry the slices of papaw until they are
crisp and brown on both sides. Slices of pumpkin
can be fried in the same way. *Note:* Papaw can be

boiled like pumpkin when it is green, and eaten as a vegetable.

PAPAW MINCE PUDDING. Take a well-developed papaw, cut a slice off the top end and take out the seeds. Into the cavity, put mincemeat mixed with finely chopped onions, salt and pepper. Tie the top back firmly, like a lid, wrap up in a cloth and boil for $\frac{3}{4}$ of an hour or, if desired, bake in an oven with a little water.

PAPAW DESSERT. Cut up a ripe papaw into cubes, add some sugar and lemon juice or a few drops of lemon essence, and stew on a slow fire for about 30 minutes. Cool thoroughly.

LOTUS LILY SOUP. This is a recipe which I obtained from the Chinese. Take the roots, which are really tubers, and clean and peel them thoroughly, as you would clean a potato. Wash them well, cut into two lengthwise, then chop into $\frac{1}{2}$-inch strips. Wash them well again. Now slice 1 lb. of lean pork very thinly and put the lily roots and the pork into a large saucepan. Mix a teaspoon of cornflour with 2 teaspoonfuls of Chinese soy sauce, a little pepper and a teaspoonful of salt. Cover with a quart of water and boil gently until the lily roots are tender.

Note: These rhizomes can be cooked in the same way as long beans, but they should be quartered lengthwise and sliced thinly. They can be served with pork or beef.

GRILLED FISH. A delicious way to grill fish is to clean it and wrap it up in wet gum leaves. Push it under the glowing coals of a wood fire. A big fish will take about half an hour to cook. When taken out, the skin and leaves will easily come away, and the flesh is ready to eat, and it is very tasty and juicy.

Select a good camp site

10

Eight, Ten, Two and a Quarter

*Eight pounds of flour, ten pounds of beef, some
sugar and some tea,
That's all they give to a hungry man until the
Seventh Day.
If you don't be moighty sparing, you'll go with
a hungry gut—
For that's one of the great misfortunes in an
old Bark Hut.*

—Old Bush Ballad.

The above ration scale is still useful as a basis for
camping supplies, and we always reckon our supplies
on it. One person going away for one week needs:

8 lb flour
10 lbs. beef
¼ lb. tea
2 lbs. sugar.

To these are added baking powder, jam, rice, vegetables, etc.

For a number of people, it is best to buy flour
in 50-lb. calico bags—and see that you buy the
double-bagged kind for a long trip; it lasts better.

A safe and simple formula to follow when you are
going bush is to write down your activities for a complete day, noting the things you are going to use. In
that way, you may be sure that you haven't left
out anything from your shopping list.

Here is a sample list:

Activities	Supplies.
You get up in the morning and— You want a wash—	Tin dish Towel Soap Razor Shaving soap Toothbrush Toothpaste
You light a fire—	Axe Matches
—and boil the billy for tea—	Billycan Tea Sugar Milk Pannikins
—and drink your tea— and eat a bit of camp-baked bread—	Flour Baking Powder Butter Jam
—and fry a bit of bacon— and add some sliced onion—	Bacon Onions Salt Frying Pan
Do the washing up—	Mop Tea towels Tin dish (al- ready checked)

And in that way, you go right through your day, thinking out the meals, and checking the various activities you expect to occupy your time, and you might finish up something like this:

It's getting dark—   Hurricane lamp
                                      Kerosene
                                      Spare wicks

—time for bed.   Bunk
                                      Mosquito Net
                                       (Axe)
                                      Blankets.

Now that is how I work all the time in the bush,
and I find that you can't go wrong. You check and
double-check all supplies. For instance, you will
write down tin dishes, matches, cups, axe and other
things several times. You need an axe to cut wood
for your first fire in the morning and you need it
again at night to cut stakes to pin down your
mosquito net.

Here is a list of cooking equipment to check against
your list:

1 10in. Bedourie camp oven.
3 billy cans with lids
A kerosene tin, for boiling the beef.
A good, strong, heavy-bottomed frying pan.
2 saucepans
3 yards of No. 10 wire to make your wire hooks.

Take a strong 10 x 12 fly rather than a tent. If
it rains, you can put bushes along the back, and also
along the front if the rain beats in. If you prefer
not to lie on the ground, take Cyclone bunks. If you
do sleep on the ground, remember to take a sheet of
thick calico, to guard against the damp. Mosquito
nets are absolutely essential, they keep out, not only
mosquitoes, but all the crawling things such as
centipedes and snakes.

Making Camp.

If possible, always pitch your camp before sundown, because you can look around the country in the daylight, select a good place, have your wood gathered and everything put ready for the night.

If it looks like rain when you are making camp, do not camp in low depressions, but on knolls, so that the rainwater will run away from your camp, not into it. See that the ground is of a sandy nature. Keep away from trees. If you are going to rig your fly on a tree, see that it is only a small stout sapling, and avoid big trees with dry limbs. Dry limbs are a sign of hollowness, and in a high wind the dry branches may come down on top of you; big trees, also, attract lightning.

See that the place for the camp is free of grass, in the event of fires, and always make your own fire in a cleared spot, on the windward side of the camp.

Look round the camping area for snake tracks or trapdoor spiders' nests. Native mothers always look very carefully, knowing that children will poke their fingers down holes. They also throw away old pieces of dry wood, which might harbour centipedes.

It is a good idea to take along a piece of 3 x 3 ark mesh, or netting, which can be put over stakes for cooking. Or, take two iron bars which can be placed across stones. A griller is useful, too.

A shovel is very necessary, for digging a trench around the camp, or around the fly in case of heavy rain. In an emergency, what is more, you can grill a good steak on the blade of a shovel.

An axe is another "must": useful for cutting away trees, bringing in timber, trimming possums and bandicoots out of trees, sharpening pegs for mosquito nets, and so on.

A folding safe is a useful item, and some people like to take a folding table. Failing the table, three or four 3-bushel corn sacks do very nicely, one for the table and the rest for chairs.

Bush First Aid.

A proper First Aid kit is really essential, but if you run out of supplies, the following simple old remedies are worth knowing:

SCORPION OR CENTIPEDE BITE. Light a match and immediately, before the phosphorescent head is burnt out, thrust it on the bite. This cauterizes the wound, and takes away infection. If you have no matches, a small firestick will do.

JELLYFISH OR BLUEBOTTLE STINGS. Rub all the stings with sand at once. Keep rubbing, until the white stings can be rolled off the skin. By doing this, the stings can be neutralized before the poison has time to act. It will still be painful, but a thorough wash with cold water can help. A blue bag, of course, is a well-known remedy, also ammonia.

STINGRAY, or other infections in the feet. The natives have a method of getting a long piece of green twine, soaking it in water and then putting it in the ashes of the fire. When it is hot, they take it out and as soon as the patient can bear the heat, bind his leg up from the ankle to the knee. This primitive hot foment certainly is very effective in neutralizing the pain of a stingray bite.

SNAKE BITE. On Groote Island, a number of people were getting bitten by death adders. As they went barefooted, the bites were almost always on the foot. The Reverend Harris, a Church of England

rector, told me that he used the following method:
He would cut deeply into the bite, and then he
would wait. The poison would gradually travel up
the vein, and form a lump. The native would show
him where the pain was, and he would cut again
at that point and squeeze out the poison and jellified
blood. He would repeat this treatment three or four
times, by which time all the poison would be out.

SORE EYES. The native mothers used to squirt milk
into their children's eyes, and this seemed to neutral-
ize the infection.

When a fly bites you in the eye, as is common in
the bush, try this simple cure: spit on your index
finger, throw your head back, and rub the spittle
slowly round the eye. Do this two or three times. It
has often been proved effective, and in many inst-
ances takes away both the pain and the risk of
infection.

COLIC, pains in the stomach. The red young tips of
the gum tree, plucked off and eaten, relieve pain in
the stomach. The basic ingredient, "crude eucalyptus," is the medicine.

HEADACHE. Finely grind the charcoal from your
fire, mix a teaspoonful with water and drink it.

WARM PACKS OR FOMENTS. A good bush remedy,
used by the Aborigines, is to heat a stone or ant-bed,
wrap it carefully in damp grass and place it on the
painful spot.

Just before we leave the subject of camping, here
are a few more hints that are worth knowing:

BUSH STRING. That is wonderful for general utility
work around the camp, such as tying flies down or
tying up mosquito nets, or even for binding primitive

bark splints on broken limbs. It is made from the inner bast of the sandy wattle tree, the cotton tree or the kurrajong. Peeled off, it is excellent string. It can be twisted into thin string or left wide like a bandage, depending on the use to which it is to be put. Some blade grasses make a good string, and so do many of the imported weeds which are varieties of fibres.

TO MAKE A FIRE ON A WET DAY. Strip the bark off a stringy bark tree on the opposite side from the weather; a dry tree is preferable, but a green one will do. Strip off the outer bark with a knife and cut out the inner bark. Now, select a dry tree and cut out of it the slabs of dry wood which can be split up. Now roll the bark between your hands, and build a small fire of tiny sticks from the dry wood. Put a match under the roll of bark in your hand and, when it is alight, put it under the pile of small sticks. They will light, because they are dry, and once your fire is well alight, you are able to burn wet wood.

HOW TO TELL SMOKE FROM CLOUDS. This is an Aboriginal method. A black cloud in the distance may be a bushfire. Keeping your eyes on it, turn your head slowly from side to side. If it is a cloud, it will remain the same; if it is smoke from a bushfire, it will seem to turn black.

A BUSH WARMING-PAN. Dig a hole at the foot of your swag, and in this put a few shovelfuls of red-hot coals. Cover with earth, and press well down. Lay the "feet" end of your swag over this.

A BURKETOWN MOSQUITO NET. Drink a bottle of O.P. rum with swamp-water.

A SHORT PRIMER

Some Australian words have a distinct flavor, too.
Here are some that were used in this book:

BANDICOOT: A small marsupial, nocturnal and omnivorous in habit.

BEE-BREAD: Pollen stored by bees for food.

BILARNEY: Name given to Bill Harney by the Australian Aborigines.

BILLABONG: A small lake remaining in the bend of a dried-up stream.

BILLY or BILLY CAN: The indispensable tin can, about the size of a 3-pound coffee can and often having a metal handle and spout, in which a bushman boils water and makes his tea.

BUSH: A rural area commonly regarded as remote from civilization.

COBBER: A friend, a mate, no matter what.

CONDY'S CRYSTALS: A potassium permanate-maganate crystal used as an antiseptic for skin abrasions.

CORNFLOUR: Cornstarch.

COVE: Slang term for a bloke, a guy, a man, or a sport.

CYCAD PALM: A fernlike palm, chiefly of the Southern Hemisphere, which produces sage, a farina-like substance.

DAMPER: The bushman's unleavened bread.

DUGONG: A sea-cow or aquatic mammal up to 8-ft. long, whose nutritious flesh resembles pork or veal.

ENO'S SALTS: Similar to alka-seltzer, in a powder form.

EPSOM SALTS: A magnesium sulfate often used as a purge.

FIRESTICK: Literally, a stick from the burning campfire.

FLYING FOX: A fruit bat whose body is about 30 cm. long.

GEORGINA: A river flowing in the border area of the Northern Territory and the state of Queensland.

GIDGEE: A small close-grained acacia tree which gives off an unpleasant odor at the approach of rain, hence sometimes called stinking wattle.

GOANNA: A large lizard, 5-6 feet long.

GOLDEN SYRUP: A canned syrup similar to light Karo syrup, processed from sugar cane and sweeter in taste. Used as a topping as well as ingredient in cooking.

LEICHHARDT: Early Australian explorer of Prussian origin, who in 1843 found an overland route from Sydney in the state of New South Wales to Moreton Bay in the state of Queensland.

MINCE: Ground beef. Or, a cooked dish including gravy and vegetables.

NARK: A general nuisance and aggravation. A spoil sport.

OUTBACK: The outer bush country, 'out-in-back' of any settled areas, generally regarded as being 'back of beyond', in aborigine country.

PANNIKIN: A small saucepan.

RISSOLE: A sausage-like fried roll consisting of mince or fish and seasonings, sometimes encased in a thin puff pastry.

ROCK CAKES: A large cookie or small cake baked with currants and almonds.

SCONE: A slightly sweetened version of our baking powder biscuit.

STATION: A ranch or large country property.

SWAG: A backpack or bushman's bundle of necessities.

TREPANG: A sea cucumber or sea slug, of the echinoderm family. A Chinese delicacy.

TUCKER: Food.

WITCHETTY GRUB: A large white grub that is the larva of the moth of the genus Cossus, which frequents the roots and trunks of Australian acacia trees. Relished by Australian Aborigines as food.

Melville Is.

Bathurst Is.

DARWIN

Timor

Sea

Oenpelli

ARNHEM LAND

Daly R.

Katherine

Roper R.

Gro

Eu

Mataranka

Victoria R.

Manangoora

Borroloola

Top Springs

Wave
Hill
Cattle Stn.

Anthony
Lagoon

S
E
C

WESTERN AUSTRALIA

Tennant

NORTHERN

TERRITORY

Alice Sprin

Ayers
Rock

Thursday Is.

Coral

Sea

Gulf of

Serpentaria

Wellesley Is.

Mitchell R.

Van
Rook
Cattle
Stn.

Mt
Molloy

Cairns

Burketown

Townsville

Lake

Charters Towers

andangie

R.

QUEENSLAND

Sketch Map of North Australia

0   100   200   300

Miles

Hawthorn Prints

AUSTRALIAN ANIMAL AND BIRD PRINTS
BY PETER HAWTHORN

The unique Australian fauna comes to life with the fine detail in these 16 black and white prints by Peter Hawthorn. Printed in Australia on high quality goatskin paper, the authenticity of the original pen and ink drawings was verified by the zoologist-director of a famed wildlife sanctuary in Healesville, Victoria, Australia.

Included are:

Platypus	13½'' x 18''
Wombat	''
Numbat	''
Spotted Cuscus (possum)	''
Leadbeaters Possum	''
Koala	13½'' x 16½''
Ringtail Possum	''
Greater Glider Possum	13½'' x 18''
'' Female & Baby	13½'' x 16½''
Grey Kangaroo	17'' x 21½''
Echidna	13½'' x 18''
Frilled-neck Lizard	''
Australian Pelican	''
Kookaburra	''
Superb Lyrebird	17'' x 21½''
Sulphur-crested Cockatoo	''

AUSTRALIAN ANIMAL AND BIRD PRINTS
are available at $6.00 each including
shipping. Please allow 2-6 weeks for
delivery:

Hawthorn Prints

COBBERS PRESS
Martensen Company Inc.
22725 Orchard Lake Road
Farmington, Michigan 48024

Dear Sirs:

Please send ____ of each of these prints:

_____

_____

_____

to me at this address: (please print)

_____

_____

_____

I enclose $_____ in check or money order.
Michigan residents please add 4% to total.

International copyrights held by the artist.

LET US HEAR FROM YOU......

More copies of these YARNS? Visit
your local bookstore or order from us.

If you want to receive more information
about our Australian publications as it
becomes available, do send us your name:

COBBERS PRESS
Martensen Company Inc.
22725 Orchard Lake Road
Farmington, Michigan 48024

Dear Cobber,

Please include my name in your list of
those interested in receiving information
about your Australian publications

_____(tick)

Please send ___ copies of YARNS FROM
AN AUSSIE BUSHCOOK @ $5.00 each
including postage. I enclose $____ .
Michigan residents add 4% sales tax
or 20¢ per copy.

        Name: _____

        Address: _____

                  _____

With an Aborigine at
Melville Island. The
man is in a ceremonial
period when he can not
touch food so must be
fed by another.

←

Harney with Dr. Frank
Setzler of the Smith-
sonian Institute at
Yirrkala. (1948
Smithsonian-National
Geographic Expedition)

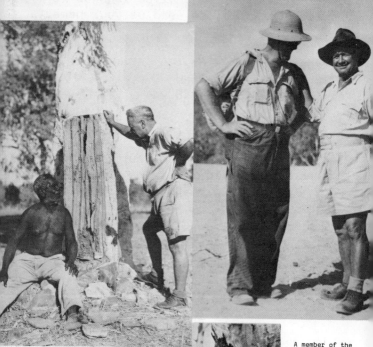

Harney interrogating
an old native near a
Leichardt memorial on
the Roper River.

↑

A member of the
Waradgery Tribe
finds a succulent
witchetty grub in
a eucalyptus tree.

←

WILLIAM E. HARNEY

Bill and anthill. ↑

In a cave at Oenpelli, West
Arnhem Land, eating flying
↓ fox with Aboriginals.

With the National Geographic
Expedition to Melville Is. 1954
↑
Front: Dr. Jane C. Goodale and
        C.P. Mountford

Back: George Joy, Brian Daly,
        and Bill Harney